IVORY COAST

IVORY COAST

William Mark Habeeb

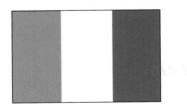

Mason Crest Publishers
Philadelphia

Produced by OTTN Publishing, Stockton, N.J.

Mason Crest Publishers
370 Reed Road
Broomall, PA 19008
www.masoncrest.com

First printing

1 3 5 7 9 8 6 4 2

Library of Congress Cataloging-in-Publication Data

Habeeb, William Mark, 1955-
  Ivory Coast / William Mark Habeeb.
     p. cm. — (Africa)
  Includes bibliographical references and index.
  ISBN 1-59084-808-X
  1. Côte d'Ivoire—Juvenile literature. I. Title. II. Series.

  DT545.22.H33 2004
  966.68—dc22

          79p. $21 95   21 cm.   2004007107

Africa:
Facts and Figures

Burundi

**Democratic Republic
of the Congo**

Ethiopia

Ghana

Ivory Coast

Kenya

Nigeria

Rwanda

South Africa

Tanzania

Uganda

Zimbabwe

Table of Contents

Africa: Continent in the Balance
Robert I. Rotberg

Africa is the cradle of humankind, but for millennia it was off the familiar, beaten path of global commerce and discovery. Its many peoples therefore developed largely apart from the diffusion of modern knowledge and the spread of technological innovation until the 17th through 19th centuries. With the coming to Africa of the book, the wheel, the hoe, and the modern rifle and cannon, foreigners also brought the vastly destructive transatlantic slave trade, oppression, discrimination, and onerous colonial rule. Emerging from that crucible of European rule, Africans created nationalistic movements and then claimed their numerous national independences in the 1960s. The result is the world's largest continental assembly of new countries.

There are 53 members of the African Union, a regional political grouping, and 48 of those nations lie south of the Sahara. Fifteen of them, including mighty Ethiopia, are landlocked, making international trade and economic growth that much more arduous and expensive. Access to navigable rivers is limited, natural harbors are few, soils are poor and thin, several countries largely consist of miles and miles of sand, and tropical diseases have sapped the strength and productivity of innumerable millions. Being landlocked, having few resources (although countries along Africa's west coast have tapped into deep offshore petroleum and gas reservoirs), and being beset by malaria, tuberculosis, schistosomiasis, AIDS, and many other maladies has kept much of Africa poor for centuries.

Thirty-two of the world's poorest 44 countries are African. Hunger is common. So is rapid deforestation and desertification. Unemployment rates are often over 50 percent, for jobs are few—even in agriculture. Where Africa once

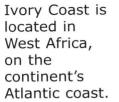

Ivory Coast is located in West Africa, on the continent's Atlantic coast.

was a land of small villages and a few large cities, with almost everyone engaged in growing grain or root crops or grazing cattle, camels, sheep, and goats, today more than half of all the more than 750 million Africans, especially those who live south of the Sahara, reside in towns and cities. Traditional agriculture hardly pays, and a number of countries in Africa—particularly the smaller and more fragile ones—can no longer feed themselves.

There is not one Africa, for the continent is full of contradictions and variety. Of the 675 million people living south of the Sahara, at least 130 million live in Nigeria, 67 million in Ethiopia, 55 million in the Democratic Republic of the Congo, and 45 million in South Africa. By contrast, tiny Djibouti and Equatorial Guinea have fewer than 1 million people each, and prosperous

A member of the Dan tribe dances in Guessesso.

Botswana and Namibia each are under 2 million in population. Within some countries, even medium-sized ones like Zambia (11 million), there are a plethora of distinct ethnic groups speaking separate languages. Zambia, typical with its multitude of competing entities, has 70 such peoples, roughly broken down into four language and cultural zones. Three of those languages jostle with English for primacy.

Given the kaleidoscopic quality of African culture and deep-grained poverty, it is no wonder that Africa has developed economically and politically less rapidly than other regions. Since independence from colonial rule, weak governance has also plagued Africa and contributed significantly to the widespread poverty of its peoples. Only Botswana and offshore Mauritius have been governed democratically without interruption since independence. Both are among Africa's wealthiest countries, too, thanks to the steady application of good governance.

Aside from those two nations, and South Africa, Africa has been a continent of coups since 1960, with massive and oil-rich Nigeria suffering incessant periods of harsh, corrupt, autocratic military rule. Nearly every other country on or around the continent, small and large, has been plagued by similar bouts of instability and dictatorial rule. In the 1970s and 1980s Idi Amin ruled Uganda capriciously and Jean-Bedel Bokassa proclaimed himself emperor of the Central African Republic. Macias Nguema of Equatorial Guinea was another in that same mold. More recently Daniel arap Moi held Kenya in thrall and Robert Mugabe has imposed himself on once-prosperous Zimbabwe. In both of those cases, as in the case of Gnassingbe Eyadema in Togo and the late Mobutu Sese Seko in Congo, these presidents stole wildly and drove entire peoples and their nations into penury. Corruption is common in Africa, and so are a weak rule-of-law framework, misplaced development, high expenditures on soldiers and low expenditures on health and education, and a widespread (but not universal) refusal on the part of leaders to work well for their followers and citizens.

Conflict between groups within countries has also been common in Africa. More than 12 million Africans have been killed in the civil wars of Africa since 1990, with more than 3 million losing their lives in Congo and more than 2 million in the Sudan. War between north and south has been constant in the Sudan since 1981. In 2003 there were serious ongoing hostilities in northeastern Congo, Burundi, Angola, Liberia, Guinea, Ivory Coast, the Central African Republic, and Guinea-Bissau, and a coup (later reversed) in São Tomé and Príncipe.

Despite such dangers, despotism, and decay, Africa is improving. Botswana and Mauritius, now joined by South Africa, Senegal, Kenya, and Ghana, are beacons of democratic growth and enlightened rule. Uganda and Senegal are taking the lead in combating and reducing the spread of AIDS, and others are following. There are serious signs of the kinds of progressive economic policy changes that might lead to prosperity for more of Africa's peoples. The trajectory in Africa is positive.

Ivory Coast has beautiful beaches but no natural harbors. (Opposite) A sandy, tree-lined beach near Grand Bassam. (Right) This view of Abidjan shows skyscrapers as well as the ornate structure of St. Paul's Cathedral.

1 Geography

BONJOUR! ARE YOU ready to discover Ivory Coast? Most of the people who live in this West African nation might greet visitors in French, the country's official language. Others might greet tourists with the word *dansi*, which means "hello" in the Dioula language, one of dozens of different native languages spoken in the country.

Ivory Coast (in French, Côte d'Ivoire) is a medium-sized country that is slightly larger than the state of New Mexico. The entire southern border of Ivory Coast is formed by the Gulf of Guinea, which is part of the Atlantic Ocean. Along the coast are beautiful beaches, which are known for their strong surf and dangerous tides. Much of the 320-mile-long (515-kilometer-long) coastline is made up of salty, shallow **lagoons** that are connected to the Gulf of Guinea by narrow canals.

Quick Facts: The Geography of Ivory Coast

Location: western Africa, bordering the Atlantic Ocean

Area: (slightly larger than New Mexico)
   total: 124,502 square miles (322,460 sq. km)
   land: 122,780 square miles (318,000 sq. km)
   water: 1,722 square miles (4,460 sq. km)

Borders: Burkina Faso, 363 miles (584 km); Ghana, 415 miles (668 km); Guinea, 379 miles (610 km); Liberia, 445 miles (716 km); Mali, 331 miles (532 km); coastline, 320 miles (515 km).

Climate: tropical, with hot temperatures and a long rainy season.

Terrain: mostly flat, with rolling hills in the north and mountains in the far west.

Elevation extremes:
   lowest point: Gulf of Guinea (sea level)
   highest point: Mt. Nimba, 5,748 feet (1,752 meters)

Natural hazards: heavy surf along coast; possible flooding during rainy season; *harmattan* wind from the north.

Source: CIA World Factbook, 2003.

In the west, Ivory Coast is bordered by Guinea and Liberia, and the terrain here features rolling hills and a few taller mountains. Ivory Coast's highest peak, Mt. Nimba, rises 5,748 feet (1,752 meters) along the border with Guinea. To the north, Ivory Coast is bordered by Mali and Burkina Faso, and on the east by Ghana.

The central part of the country is a mostly flat *plateau*, and is the main farming region for coffee and cocoa, Ivory Coast's most important crops. The northern half of the country is *savanna*, an area of rolling hills, low-lying vegetation, and only scattered trees. Three long rivers—the Sassandra, the Bandama, and the Comoe—run almost the entire length of Ivory Coast from north to south, draining into the Gulf of Guinea. Both the Sassandra and Bandama have been dammed to generate *hydroelectric* power.

Tropical Climate

Ivory Coast is located just 400 miles (644 km) north of the *equator*, which gives the country a tropical climate throughout the year. Only the mountainous areas in the far western part of Ivory Coast enjoy periodic cool temperatures.

The country's location near the equator also means that Ivory Coast receives about 12 hours of daylight all year long, and does not experience the four seasons typical of more northern or more southern climates. Ivory Coast has three seasons, which are determined by the amount of rainfall received in each. From November to March, weather throughout the country is generally warm and dry. From March to May, the weather is hot and dry. From May to November it is hot, humid, and very rainy. During this season flooding is common in some areas, particularly around the Sassandra, Bandama, and Comoe rivers and along the frontier with Liberia. The coastal areas receive abundant rainfall all year.

Most of the country experiences little variation in temperature. In Abidjan, which is located along the coast, the average high temperature is between 80° and 90° Fahrenheit (27° and 32° Celsius) year round, and the humidity is almost always over 90 percent, even during the dry season. Evening temperatures in Abidjan rarely drop below 70° F (22° C). In the northern parts of Ivory Coast, daytime temperatures regularly soar to near 100° F (38° C), especially during the dry season. In the mountainous western area, temperatures can dip as low as 60° F (16° C) at night, although daytime temperatures usually are between 80° and 85° F (26° and 30° C).

From December through February, a hot wind known as the *harmattan* blows south from the distant Sahara Desert into the northern regions of Ivory Coast. Some years, the *harmattan* is so strong that visibility is reduced and daily life becomes a miserable struggle against blowing sand and dust. The *harmattan* can be strong enough to blow down trees, and can make working in the fields almost impossible for farmers. Dust clouds stirred up by this hot wind can also make breathing difficult, forcing people to stay indoors.

Other than the *harmattan* and occasional flooding, Ivory Coast is generally free from major natural hazards such as tropical storms or hurricanes.

Plants and Wildlife

Much of the dense rain forest that once covered more than half of southern and central Ivory Coast has been cleared for timber, making way for large-scale agriculture (particularly for the cultivation of such crops as coffee and cocoa). Expansive groves of palm trees cover much of the coastal areas, and are exploited for their valuable palm oil. In the vast grasslands of northern Ivory Coast, low-lying bushes and trees, such as the acacia, are the primary forms of plant life.

In an effort to save the disappearing rainforests—which today cover only 7 percent of the country—Ivory Coast established the Tai National Park to preserve one of the last remaining virgin rainforests in all of West Africa. Located in the far southwestern corner of Ivory Coast, near the border with Liberia, the Tai National Park covers about 1,400 square miles (3,600 sq. km). A visit to Tai is like a journey back in time—the park is filled with huge trees,

Leopards can be found in the Tai National Park, which is located in the southwestern part of Ivory Coast.

hanging vines, exotic flowers, and cool streams, and these give visitors an idea of what all of southern Ivory Coast looked like centuries ago. The park is also home to a large number of chimpanzees, as well as hippopotamus, buffalo, antelopes, leopards, many species of monkey, and over 200 types of birds. Because of the rainforest's delicate environment, the number of visitors allowed into the park is strictly controlled.

In all, Ivory Coast has nearly 5,000 species of plants, over 200 species of mammals, and various types of lizards and poisonous snakes, making the country's *biodiversity* among the richest in the world. Ivory Coast's bird life is particularly fascinating. Over 500 species have been recorded, including some that are *indigenous* to Ivory Coast, like the Nimba Fly Catcher.

The Park Comoe, in the northeastern corner of Ivory Coast, is the largest game park in West Africa. It is home to lions, antelopes, baboons, and a large herd of elephants. Elephants once roamed throughout Ivory Coast. In fact, the region began to be called "the ivory coast" in the 17th century because it was a center for trade in the valuable ivory from elephant tusks.

(Opposite) This child is a member of the Baoulé tribe, one of the many ethnic groups that share Ivory Coast. (Right) This photograph from the 1930s shows the remains of a palace that once belonged to one of Ivory Coast's kings. The authority of African chiefs was limited after the 19th century, as much of Ivory Coast came under French control.

2 History

IVORY COAST'S HISTORY is similar to that of many African states. During the 19th century, Europeans imposed national borders on an area that encompassed a collection of various ethnic groups. France controlled Ivory Coast as a colony, but during the 1940s and 1950s the native people struggled for independence under the guidance of a strong and *charismatic* leader. Upon achieving independence in 1960, Ivory Coast initially prospered economically and enjoyed political stability, but in recent years the country has had to confront mounting economic problems, ethnic conflict, and civil war.

Earliest Inhabitants

Not much is known about the earliest inhabitants of the region today known as Ivory Coast. Written reports indicate that by the 11th century

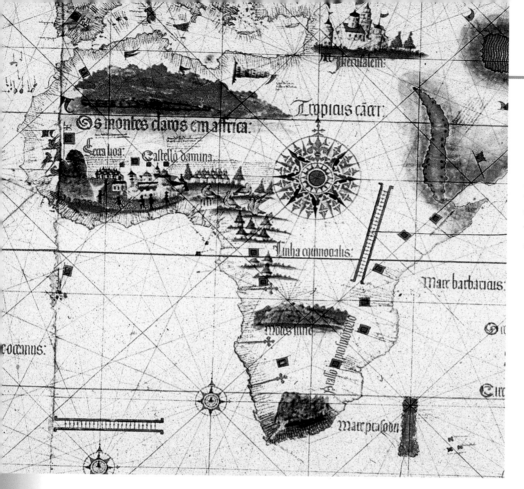

This detail from a Portuguese map drawn in 1501 shows Portuguese settlements and trading posts along the coast of Africa. These are marked with flags.

Muslim traders from northern and eastern Africa had made their way into the northern regions of Ivory Coast, but they were halted by the dense rainforest that covered the southern portion of the country at that time. These traders found a collection of isolated farming communities that had very little contact with the outside world, or even with each other. The rain forest made communication between villages difficult.

After the 15th century, various *ethnic groups* from neighboring areas started *migrating* to Ivory Coast. The Kru people came from the region today known as Liberia; the Lubi and Senoufo people migrated south from Burkina Faso and Mali; the Baoulé people entered Ivory Coast from Ghana; and the Malinke migrated from Guinea. These migrations lasted for over 200 years, and Ivory Coast's current population consists primarily of descendents of these migrants. Each of these groups established local kingdoms in the areas where they settled.

Portuguese explorers began sailing along the coast of West Africa in the 15th century, and became the first modern Europeans to chart the coasts of Ivory Coast. In other parts of West Africa, the Portuguese established settlements and trading posts so that they could trade for valuable commodities such as gold and spices with Africans. By the 16th century, among the "commodities" sold in these trading posts were human beings. Slaves were needed to work in European colonies in North and South America, and the African slave trade flourished along the coast of West Africa.

The people of Ivory Coast were relatively untouched by the inhumanity of the slave trade, however. There were no sheltered harbors on the coast, and this made it impractical for Europeans to establish permanent trading posts. As a result, the inhabitants of Ivory Coast initially had very little direct contact with Europeans.

Natives of the area did want to trade for European goods, and this would have a terrible impact on the region's elephant population. Europeans were interested in acquiring elephant ivory, and during the 17th century a profitable trade in ivory developed. In fact, this much-prized resource gave the region its name. However, by the early 18th century hunters had virtually wiped out the entire elephant population in Ivory Coast.

French Colonization

Portugal's control over West Africa was gradually eclipsed by the rise of other European powers. France in particular gained a great deal of influence in West Africa, establishing its first settlement in Senegal in the mid-17th century. In 1687 the French founded the first permanent settlement in Ivory Coast, a *mission* at Assini. Despite this foothold, the French did not establish themselves firmly in Ivory Coast until the mid-19th century.

In the 1840s the French built a series of forts along the coast of Ivory Coast to protect French traders, who had begun dealing with local village chiefs, and to counter the British colonization of nearby Ghana. One of these forts, Grand Bassam, grew into a French administrative settlement. Throughout the second half of the 1800s France secured control over the coast and gradually pushed inland as well. French settlers followed and began cultivating cocoa, coffee, bananas, and palm oil for export back to France.

By the late 1800s, such major European powers as Great Britain, France, Belgium, and Germany were in fierce competition for control over Africa and access to the continent's valuable raw materials. In order to avoid potential conflict, representatives of the colonial powers met in Berlin in 1884–85 to decide how to divide Africa among themselves. Each of the countries was given control over the parts of Africa in which they had established their colonial authority. At this conference France was granted much of western and central Africa, including Ivory Coast.

While the Berlin Conference was successful in preventing colonial wars among the European powers, it also created artificial boundaries throughout

European leaders met at the Berlin Conference in 1884–85 to divide up control over Africa. Because the French had already established themselves in West Africa, the conference granted them control over the area that today is Ivory Coast.

Africa. The boundaries frequently divided members of the same ethnic group between two or more countries, or brought ethnic groups that had been traditional enemies into the same country. When they redrew the map of Africa, the Europeans gave no consideration to the needs or desires of the African people.

At Berlin, and in subsequent meetings among the European powers, the boundaries of Ivory Coast were **delineated**. The other European powers recognized it as a French possession. In 1893, Ivory Coast officially became a French colony, with the coastal town of Grand Bassam as its capital.

But the French conquest of Ivory Coast did not come easily. Thousands of French soldiers were sent deep into the countryside to subdue the local African population, most of whom fought back fiercely against French control. A powerful leader named Samory Touré led the resistance to French authority during the 1880s and 1890s. The French did not fully control Ivory Coast until they defeated Touré's Malinke forces in the late 1890s, and Baoulé insurgents in 1917.

The Africans especially disliked the French policy of forced labor, in which Africans were made to work on the farms and *plantations* of the French settlers, or in building roads and railroad lines for the colonial government. They received little or no pay for their labor.

Many West Africans were forced to fight for France in Europe during World War I (1914–1918), which only increased their resentment when they returned home and were once again required to work for the French. "The public works programs undertaken by the Ivorian colonial government and the exploitation of natural resources required massive commitments of labor," writes Robert E. Handloff in *Ivory Coast: A Country Study*. "The French therefore imposed a system of forced labor under which each male adult Ivorian was required to work for ten days each year without compensation as part of his obligation to the state. The system was subject to extreme misuse and was the most hated aspect of French colonial rule."

After France surrendered to Nazi Germany during World War II, Ivoirians saw an opportunity to demand an end to colonialism. One of their leaders was a charismatic cocoa farmer and medical doctor named Félix Houphouet-Boigny. In 1944, he formed a union for Ivorian farmers to protest against French policies such as forced labor. Although Houphouet-Boigny was the son of a Baoulé chief, he also was a Roman Catholic who became a French citizen. In 1945 Houphouet-Boigny was elected to the French Parliament in Paris, where he continued to speak out against French colonial policies. In 1946, France abolished the practice of forced labor and offered French citizenship to all of Ivory Coast's residents.

In part because of the pressure of African leaders like Houphouet-Boigny, France gradually accepted that its direct control over Ivory Coast and its other West African colonies would have to end. In 1958, France implemented the Overseas Reform Act, which transferred many powers formerly held by France to local African governments in each of its colonies. In 1958, Ivory Coast became an *autonomous* republic as a member of the French Community, an organization that France established to try and maintain its influence and indirect control over its colonies.

Independence

In August 1960, following the lead of other former French colonies in West Africa, Ivory Coast withdrew from the French Community and declared itself an independent country. On October 31, 1960, the National Assembly of Ivory Coast adopted a constitution establishing an independent republic. Houphouet-Boigny was elected Ivory Coast's first president.

Houphouet-Boigny knew that the most difficult task he would face would be maintaining a sense of Ivorian nationality in a country that was composed of people who were members of many different ethnic groups. The borders of most African countries had been determined by Europeans in the 19th century,

These West African leaders were photographed together in France during June 1960, a few moments after asking French president Charles DeGaulle about independence for their countries. They are (left to right) Hubert Maga of Dahomey (present-day Benin), Maurice Yameogo of Upper Volta (present-day Burkina Faso), Félix Houphouet-Boigny of Ivory Coast, and Hamani Diori of Niger. In August 1960, Ivory Coast withdrew from the French Community and became an independent nation; the other West African countries also gained independence around the same time.

and were based on the areas each country ruled during the colonial period. As a result, the African countries were, in a sense, "artificial" states. Many Ivoirians had family members in neighboring countries with whom they had more in common than they did with their own fellow Ivorian citizens. For example, the Malinke ethnic group, who live mostly in the western part of Ivory Coast, is also one of the major ethnic groups of neighboring Guinea.

Houphouet-Boigny helped to keep Ivory Coast unified by promoting economic growth. He poured money and resources into expanding the coffee, sugar, and cocoa bean farms that the French had established. Before long, Ivory Coast was one of the world's leading producers of coffee and sugar. In 1979, it became the world's number-one producer of cocoa, which is used to make chocolate. Ivory Coast also was Africa's leading exporter of pineapples and palm oil. Because the international prices of both coffee and cocoa rose steadily throughout the 1970s, Ivory Coast's wealth also grew, to the point that it was one of the most affluent countries in Africa. People around the world referred to Ivory Coast's economic success as "the Ivorian miracle." The country's prosperity helped to maintain a peaceful society.

But Houphouet-Boigny also ruled in a very *authoritarian* manner. Only one political party was permitted, and the only name that ever appeared on the ballot during presidential elections was that of Houphouet-Boigny. The press was not free to criticize the government, and opposition leaders were either jailed or expelled from the country. Houphouet-Boigny spent millions of dollars turning the village where he was born, Yamoussoukro, into a modern capital city with a huge presidential palace and other government buildings, as well as hotels, an airport, and one of the largest Roman Catholic cathedrals in the world. The capital was officially transferred from Abidjan to Yamoussoukro in 1983, although many Ivoirians regarded the construction of the new capital as a waste of money.

The "Ivorian miracle" began to unravel during the 1980s. The world prices of sugar, coffee, and cocoa are established by international demand for these products, and when the demand declined, prices fell. Ivorians were making less money and unemployment rose. Students and workers led protests in the streets, some of which turned violent.

Eventually, the pressure forced Houphouet-Boigny to allow other political parties to participate in elections. In the 1990 presidential election Houphouet-Boigny faced an opponent for the first time. He still won with 85 percent of the vote, but the era of one-party rule had come to an end.

Ivory Coast After Houphouet-Boigny

Houphouet-Boigny ruled Ivory Coast until 1993, when he died at age 88. His successor, Henri Konan Bédié, had been a supporter and ally of Houphouet-Boigny. He was also a member of the same ethnic group (the Baoulé) and was a Christian. After Bedie won the 1995 presidential election—in part by preventing the leading opposition candidate from running—he tried to tighten his grip on the government by sending opposition leaders to jail and otherwise suppressing political activity. In 1999, Bedie declared once again that the leading opposition candidate—Alassane Ouattara, a Muslim from a different ethnic group—would not be allowed to run in the forthcoming elections in 2000.

In December 1999, before the elections could be held, Bédié was ousted in a military coup led by General Robert Guëï. This sparked several years of political chaos that have still not fully been resolved. Guëï tried to hold onto power himself, but was forced to hold presidential elections in October 2000. Although Guëï tried to rig the election, the people elected Laurent Gbagbo, a *socialist* and long-time opposition leader. The election was controversial, and not everyone accepted the outcome. Because Ouattara had not been permitted to run for president, his supporters—mostly Muslims in the northern part of the country—boycotted the vote, staged protests, and refused to recognize Gbagbo's election. Hundreds of Ivorians were killed in violence associated with the 2000 election.

Henri Konan Bédié became president of Ivory Coast in 1993 after the death of Houphouet-Boigny, but his government was overthrown in December 1999.

In September 2002, a full-scale civil war broke out between various rebel groups, supporters of Ouattara, and government forces under the control of Gbagbo. Parts of the country were overrun by rebels, some of whom came from neighboring countries such as Liberia and Sierra Leone, which were themselves in the midst of ethnic wars. France sent troops to help maintain order and to evacuate the many French citizens who worked and

Confusion reigns over Abidjan, October 2000, after the military opened fire on a crowd of Laurent Gbagbo's supporters. The crowd had been protesting attempts by the incumbent, General Robert Gueï, to invalidate the election. Hundreds of people were killed in violence associated with the 2000 election in Ivory Coast.

lived in Ivory Coast. Tragically, Ivory Coast was now in the throes of ethnic and religious conflict—the very thing Houphouet-Boigny had always tried to prevent.

Ivory Coast Today

In January 2003, Gbagbo met with leaders of the rebel groups in Paris. Both sides agreed to a truce and the formation of a new government that would include members of all of the country's *factions*. But there was still very little trust between the government and opposition forces, and by September 2003 rebel leaders had pulled out of the new government to protest actions by Gbagbo. The army threatened to resume fighting if the rebel groups turned to violence. Ivory Coast appeared once again to be headed toward civil war.

In order to prevent a return to war, the United Nations agreed in February 2004 to send a force of 6,500 peacekeeping troops to Ivory Coast to join the 4,000 French troops already there. One of the first goals of the peacekeeping mission was to try and disarm both the rebels and the government forces in order to insure that civil war would not erupt again.

In the long run, however, Ivory Coast, like many African nations, must figure out how to create a fair and equitable society composed of citizens from various ethnic groups and religions. This is no easy task in a bitterly fractured country.

Ivory Coast has maintained close ties with France since gaining independence in 1960. (Opposite) Félix Houphouet-Boigny meets with French Prime Minister Jacques Chirac in Yamoussoukro in 1986. (Right) Rebels in Bouaké demonstrate against the Gbagbo administration. In recent years Ivory Coast's government has been shaken by violence.

3 The Government of Ivory Coast

UPON ACHIEVING INDEPENDENCE in 1960, Ivory Coast established a presidential form of government modeled on the French constitution. Like the French system, the Ivorian constitution placed most political power in the hands of the president and the central government. Such a system helped to reinforce the prominent role of Félix Houphouet-Boigny, the country's independence leader and first president.

Ivory Coast's constitution provides for a strong presidency, but it gives powers to a legislature as well. This separation of powers was designed to ensure that no single branch of government could become too dominant.

The constitution, which was revised in 2000, provides for freedom of speech, assembly, and religion, as well as the right of citizens to change the government through democratic means. These rights have not always been protected or enforced, however.

The Executive Branch

The president is elected for a five-year term, and is both head of state and commander in chief of the armed forces. The president may negotiate and ratify treaties with foreign governments, and may also submit bills to the National Assembly. On important issues, the president can call for a national *referendum*, in which the people of the country are allowed to vote either in favor of or against government proposals.

The president selects the prime minister as well as members of the *cabinet*, who serve at his discretion. The prime minister is in charge of the day-to-day functions of government, and the president may give him broader powers. The prime minister also serves as the minister of planning, which means that he is in charge of directing the country's economic policies. The other cabinet ministers head various government agencies that oversee the operation of the country. These include the agriculture, foreign, and defense ministries.

The president plays the leading role on all major policy decisions, and all central government officials are ultimately responsible to the president.

The National Assembly

The National Assembly is a *unicameral* legislature composed of 225 members directly elected by the people for five-year terms that run concurrently with the presidential term. Its members are called "deputies," and each one represents, and is elected from, a single district. The president of the National Assembly, who is chosen by the deputies, is first in line to succeed the president of the country in the event the president dies in office. The assembly normally meets in Yamoussoukro for two sessions per year, each one lasting about three months. However, emergency sessions may be called by the president of the assembly or by a majority of deputies.

The assembly votes on legislation submitted to it by the president or prime minister, and can also introduce and approve legislation itself. The president of Ivory Coast can carry out many actions without needing the approval of the National Assembly, however.

Until 1990, Ivory Coast had only one political party, that of President Houphouet-Boigny. This party was the Parti Démocratique de la Côte d'Ivoire (Democratic Party of Ivory Coast, or PDCI). Every deputy in the National Assembly was a member of the PDCI, and there was no real debate.

Because of popular pressure for greater democracy in Ivory Coast, Houphouet-Boigny agreed to allow other parties to form. After his death there was a struggle for power among the different parties and factions. Representatives of six parties held seats in the National Assembly that was elected in 2000. Major political parties in Ivory Coast now include the Front Populaire Ivorienne (Ivorian People's Front, or FPI), Rassemblement des Républicains (Rally of the Republicans, or RDR), and Parti Ivorien des Travailleurs (Ivorian Workers' Party, or PIT). There are also 22 independents serving in the National Assembly. As a result of these changes, serious debate among the deputies now occurs regularly.

In the next national election both the president and members of the National Assembly will be selected. The election is scheduled to be held in 2005, unless the unresolved civil war dictates otherwise.

In Ivory Coast, as in many other African countries, different ethnic groups still revere their traditional kings, such as Nana Bonzo II, king of the Ndenye people. Although tribal rulers do not play a direct role in governing Ivory Coast, they often provide direction for their pople with regard to government policies.

The Judicial System

According to the Ivorian constitution, the judicial system is supposed to be independent, even though the president has considerable power to appoint and remove judges. The judicial system is headed by the Supreme Court and includes a Court of Appeals and a number of lower courts. A special High Court of Justice has been established to try government officials who are accused of major crimes. There is also an independent Constitutional Council, which consists of seven members, appointed by the president. This council is responsible for determining who is eligible to run for the presidency and other public offices, and for overseeing the electoral process.

The constitution allows for public trial, the right to defense, and the right to *appeal* a conviction. In some rural areas, disputes and conflicts are handled by traditional community leaders instead of by the official legal system. Members of the armed forces are tried by special military courts.

Local Government

Ivory Coast is divided into 19 regions and 58 departments. Each region and department is headed by a *prefect* who is appointed by the central government. In 2002, for the first time, voters were allowed to elect departmental councils, although these councils have limited power.

Ivory Coast has 196 municipalities, each headed by an elected mayor. The city of Abidjan has 10 mayors—one for each of the city's "communes" or regions.

Local governments are not permitted to impose taxes or collect revenue, and must therefore rely on the central government for the funds to pay their operating expenses. This means that the central government, and not the local governments, has the final say on how much public money is budgeted for each region and department, and how the money is spent.

(Opposite) Two men load crates of pineapples onto the back of a truck. Ivory Coast is one of the world's leading producers of pineapples, and agriculture is an important part of the national economy. (Right) Abidjan has the largest and most modern port in West Africa, and it has become a hub for international shipping.

4 An Economy Based on Commodities

BEFORE THE ARRIVAL OF Europeans, the various ethnic groups that lived in Ivory Coast survived primarily by *subsistence* agriculture and, along the coast, by fishing. The economy was based on the village, which was generally self-sufficient. While villages often traded goods with other villages, there was no sense of a larger national economy.

When the French arrived in the 19th century, they took advantage of Ivory Coast's tropical environment to establish large plantations to produce coffee, sugar, cocoa, pineapples, and other agricultural commodities for export to Europe. Ivorians worked on these plantations—often as forced laborers—but did not own them or benefit from their production. Many French colonists became very wealthy from the plantations, but little of this wealth ever made its way to the African people. After independence, however, Ivorians took over the former French plantations and made the export of commodities the backbone of the new country's national economy.

Ivory Coast's economy is still based on the export of tropical agricultural commodities. Today, 40 percent of the world's cocoa comes from Ivory Coast, and it remains among the world's leading producers of coffee, pineapples, and palm oil.

Nearly 70 percent of Ivory Coast's population works in agriculture, and

Cocoa and Coffee

The next time you eat a chocolate bar, drink chocolate milk, or enjoy a chocolate shake, you should think of Ivory Coast, the world's largest producer of cocoa, the primary ingredient in chocolate. In 2003, Ivory Coast produced 1.3 million tons of cocoa beans (the second-largest producer of cocoa, Ghana, produced less than 500,000 tons). Virtually all of the cocoa produced in Ivory Coast is for export, so there is a good chance you have eaten chocolate made from cocoa grown in Ivory Coast.

Cocoa trees thrive in hot and humid tropical climates, which makes Ivory Coast the ideal environment. Large pods grow on the trunks and branches of cocoa trees. When the pods are ripe, they are cut off the cocoa tree with a machete, and then split open with a knife. Inside are dozens of cocoa beans. The beans are spread out to dry in the hot sun, then bagged and shipped to processing plants in Ivory Coast or abroad. Here, through a complicated process, the beans are roasted and turned into cocoa liquor, cocoa butter, and cocoa powder—all of which are used to make chocolate confections.

Harvesting cocoa beans is extremely hard work and must be done by hand— there are no machines that can remove the pods from cocoa trees without damaging the trees, and no machines that can safely extract the valuable cocoa beans from the pods. Cocoa production is the largest industry in Ivory Coast, employing over 3.5 million workers. Most of these are independent farmers and farm families, some of who own only a handful of cocoa trees.

the sale of agricultural products provides about 29 percent of the country's *gross domestic product* (GDP)—the total value of goods and services produced in the country annually. Industries such as oil refining, food and beverage processing, and truck and bus assembly contribute about 22 percent of the country's GDP. Services, such as banking and professional businesses, make up the remainder of the country's annual gross domestic product.

Ivory Coast also produces more coffee than any other country in Africa, and is one of the largest coffee producers in the world. In 2003, Ivorian farmers produced over 200,000 tons of coffee. Coffee trees, like cocoa trees, thrive in Ivory Coast's hot climate (they would not survive a frost), and grow primarily in forested areas not far from the coast.

The coffee tree is officially a type of shrub. Coffee trees produce hundreds of small fruits that start out green and turn bright red when ripe (which is why they sometimes are called coffee "cherries"). Each cherry contains two seeds—these are the coffee beans. The average coffee tree will produce 5.5 pounds (2.5 kilograms) of coffee cherries per year, enough to make around 40 cups of coffee.

When the cherries are ripe, they are picked individually by hand—a very arduous and time-consuming process. The cherries also must be picked at just the right time. If they are harvested too early or too late, the resulting coffee will be of poor quality. The cherries are then laid on mats in the hot sun to dry, often for up to a month. They are then cracked open to obtain the two seeds inside, which are sorted, cleaned, and placed in bags for shipment. The beans are roasted at around 400° F (200° C). In some cases the roasted beans are packaged for sale, or they are ground into a coarse powder, packaged, and sold as coffee.

Neither cocoa nor coffee trees are indigenous to Ivory Coast. The French introduced both plants during the 19th century.

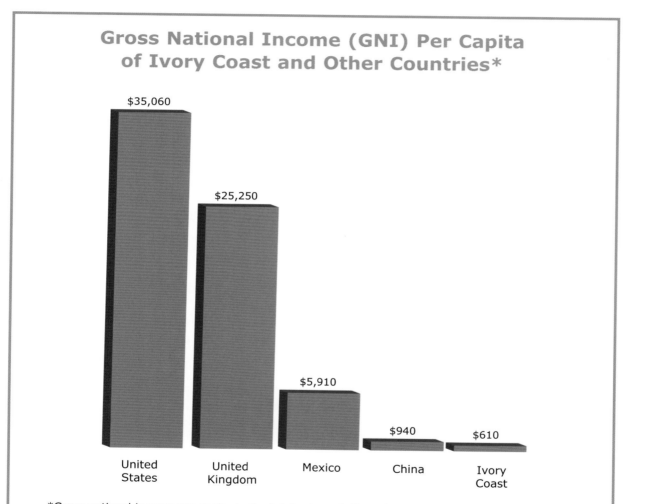

Gross National Income (GNI) Per Capita of Ivory Coast and Other Countries*

$35,060 — United States
$25,250 — United Kingdom
$5,910 — Mexico
$940 — China
$610 — Ivory Coast

*Gross national income per capita is the total value of all goods and services produced domesti-cally in a year, supplemented by income received from abroad, divided by midyear population. The above figures take into account fluctuations in currency exchange rates and differences in inflation rates across global economies.

Figures are 2002 estimates. Source: World Bank, 2003.

Instability in the Economy

Ivory Coast's revenues are dependent upon the international prices of the commodities it exports. Because a number of other countries produce the same crops, Ivory Coast's farmers have little control over the prices their products will bring on the world market. They are therefore at the mercy of fluctuations in world prices for coffee, cocoa, and other commodities. When world commodity prices are high, as they were in the 1960s and 1970s, Ivory Coast's income was relatively high. During this period, Ivory Coast had one of the fastest growing economies in all of Africa, and personal income grew steadily. But when world prices are low, as they were in the 1980s and the early 1990s, Ivory Coast's economy suffers and personal income declines.

An agriculture-based economy such as Ivory Coast's also is subject to changing weather conditions. Severe drought or flooding can cause serious damage to crops and be devastating to the economy.

One way to measure the living standard in a country is Gross National Income (GNI) per capita, which roughly measures each individual's share of the national economy. In 2002 Ivory Coast's GNI per capita was estimated at $610, which places it in the lower third of the world's nations, although it is still one of the the highest among African nations. By comparison, in 1973—when commodity prices were high and Ivory Coast was politically stable—its per capita GNI was higher than it is today, and placed the country in the top third of world nations at that time.

The decline in GNI per capita is the direct result of falling commodity prices, growing population, and the effects of political unrest and civil war. Although Ivory Coast's gross domestic product grew at a healthy rate in the second half of the 1990s—an average increase of 5 percent a year between 1996 and 1999—the violence in the country has caused GDP to decline slightly since then. As a result, in recent years Ivory Coast has experienced a level of poverty that was unknown in the 1970s and 1980s. Today, nearly 50 percent of the population of Ivory Coast survives on less than $2 per day in income.

If Ivory Coast's people are to have a better future, they must work to solve their political problems, which frighten away foreign investors, and seek ways to *diversify* their economy so that it is not so dependent upon unstable international commodity prices.

Efforts to Diversify the Economy

Since independence, the Ivorian government has tried to implement policies to diversify the economy and make it less dependent upon agriculture. These have had only limited success. With the assistance of foreign investors and economic aid, the government established factories to make textiles, fertilizer, and food products. In particular, the government tried to encourage the development of industries based on Ivory Coast's agricultural products. For example, factories were established to manufacture chocolate powder and chocolate bars, products that could be exported for more profit than cocoa beans. Similarly, instead of only exporting pineapples, factories were established to process pineapple juice for export, which would bring in more revenue than exporting the unprocessed fruit.

Under Houphouet-Boigny, Ivory Coast implemented liberal banking and

A technician checks the quality of cotton cloth produced at the Filature Tissage Gonfreville textile factory in Bouaké.

business laws that allowed Abidjan to develop into a principal African banking center and the headquarters for many major companies. Abidjan also is the headquarters of the African Development Bank, a major international organization that provides loans for economic projects throughout Africa.

The government has granted international oil companies rights to explore for offshore oil and natural gas deposits in the Gulf of Guinea, and these companies have succeeded in discovering some large deposits. As a result, Ivory Coast is today completely self-sufficient in both oil and natural gas. It has even begun to export natural gas to some neighboring countries. Some energy specialists believe that Ivory Coast has a great deal more off-shore oil and gas yet to be discovered.

Despite these efforts, however, agriculture remains Ivory Coast's major source of employment as well as the primary source of foreign income, with 85 percent of all export earnings deriving from the sale of agricultural commodities.

Modern Infrastructure

Ivory Coast took advantage of the economic boom of the 1970s to develop one of Africa's most modern and efficient *infrastructures*. Ivory Coast has an

Quick Facts: The Economy of Ivory Coast

Gross domestic product (GDP*):
$24.03 billion

Inflation: 3.2%

Natural resources: natural gas, petroleum, timber

Agriculture (29% of GDP): coffee, cocoa beans, bananas, palm kernels, corn, rice, manioc (tapioca), sweet potatoes, sugar, cotton, rubber, timber

Industry (22% of GDP): foodstuffs, beverages, wood products, oil refining, truck and bus assembly, textiles, fertilizer, building materials, electricity

Services (49% of GDP): government, banking and finance

Foreign Trade:
Exports—$4.4 billion: cocoa, coffee, timber, petroleum, cotton, bananas, pineapples, palm oil, fish
Imports—$2.5 billion: fuel, capital equipment, foodstuffs

Economic growth rate: 5.5%

Currency exchange rate: 546.49 CAF francs = U.S. $1 (June 2004)

*GDP is the total value of goods and services produced in a country annually.
All figures are 2002 estimates unless otherwise indicated.
Sources: CIA World Factbook, 2003; Bloomberg.com.

excellent road system, with more than 8,000 miles of paved roads. Its telecommunications network is one of the best in Africa, and includes a public data communications network, cellular telephone system, and widespread internet access. This network of roads and modern communications facilities remains one of the country's most important economic assets.

Abidjan has the largest and most modern seaport in all of West Africa. The port was created in 1951, when the French built the Vridi Canal, which connected the lagoons around the city with the Gulf of Guinea and gave Abidjan access to the Atlantic Ocean for the first time. Abidjan's international airport is a busy hub serving the entire region with daily flights to many European capitals. A number of European and American companies, such as Citibank, have established operations in Abidjan because of the easy access it offers to the rest of the continent.

Fortunately, the economic crisis and civil war that wracked Ivory Coast in 2002 and 2003 caused little physical damage to the country's infrastructure. It did, however, delay government investment on upkeep and modernization, and drove some foreign companies out of the country. If Ivory Coast can return to political stability and internal peace, its strong infrastructure assets should make it an attractive country for investment and commerce.

(Opposite) Women from the Senoufo tribe use traditional tools to grind grain in Guefienkaha. (Right) Baoulé men wear carved masks during a ceremony in the Man region.

5 Culture and People

IVORY COAST IS A YOUNG country. It did not exist until the late 19th century, and it did not become independent until 1960. Today, the many tribal and ethnic groups that inhabit Ivory Coast consider themselves Ivorians and are proud of their country. But they also maintain a strong allegiance to their particular traditions and religious beliefs. This gives Ivory Coast a dynamic and diverse cultural life, but has also been the cause of tension and conflict.

Members of more than 60 different ethnic groups live in Ivory Coast, speaking dozens of different languages or language dialects, and having their own unique traditions, cultures, and legends. Like most African nations, Ivory Coast's boundaries were drawn by Europeans. As a result, virtually every ethnic group in Ivory Coast has members who live in neighboring countries. It is not unusual for an Ivorian to have more in common culturally and *linguistically* with a resident of Guinea, Ghana, or Mali than he does with other Ivorians.

Ethnic Diversity

Ivory Coast has four main ethnic groups—the Akan, Kru, Voltaic, and Mande—which can be subdivided into dozens of smaller groups. The largest single ethnic group in Ivory Coast is known as the Akan. These people migrated from the central forest region of Ghana during the 17th and 18th centuries. Akan-speaking peoples account for more than 40 percent of the population of Ivory Coast.

Within the Akan, the largest tribal subgroup is the Baoulé, who account for around 15 percent of the country's population. Many Baoulé left the Ghana region because of a conflict between rival chiefs the powerful Asante Kingdom in the late 17th century, although some Baoulé still live in Ghana. The Baoulé are known for their efficient and productive farming traditions. Since the 1950s, many of Ivory Coast's political leaders have been Baoulé.

Groups that speak Voltaic languages and migrated to Ivory Coast from the north make up about 18 percent of Ivory Coast's population. One of the largest of these subgroups is the Senoufo, who make up about 10 percent of the total population. The Voltaic groups live primarily in the northeastern regions of Ivory Coast.

The Kru originally lived in what is today Liberia; they make up around 11 percent of the population. The Kru were probably the first people to migrate into Ivory Coast, and today most live in the southwestern part of the

Quick Facts: The People of Ivory Coast

Population: 16,962,491

Ethnic groups: Akan (including Baoulé), 42%; Voltaic, or Gur, 18%; Northern Mandes, 16%; Kru, 11%; Southern Mandes, 10%; other (includes Lebanese and French), 3%

Age structure:
0–14 years: 45.4%
15–64 years: 52.4%
65 years and over: 2.2%

Birth rate: 40.01 births/1,000 population

Infant mortality rate: 98.33 deaths/1,000 live births

Death rate: 18.41 deaths/ 1,000 population

Population growth rate: 2.15%

Life expectancy at birth:
total population: 42.65 years
male: 40.34 years
female: 45.04 years

Total fertility rate: 5.51 children born/woman

Religions: Traditional indigenous, 40%; Muslim, 40%; Christian, 20%

Languages: French (official); 60 other languages and dialects spoken

Literacy: 50.9%

All figures are 2003 estimates.
Source: Adapted from CIA World Factbook, 2003.

country. The largest of the Kru groups is the Bété, many of whom have converted to Christianity. The Bété have historically opposed the political domination of Ivory Coast by the Baoulé. In 1970, a Bété leader named Gnagbé Niabé (also known as Gnabé Opadjelé) led a short-lived rebellion against Houphouet-Boigny's administration, which ended when he was captured by government troops.

The Mande live in the northwestern area of Ivory Coast and along the border with Mali. Subgroups include the Malinke and the Dan, as well as other related ethnic groups. They are known as skillful traders and also are an important ethnic group in neighboring Guinea and Mali.

Not all Ivorians are of African descent. About 100,000 Lebanese live in Ivory Coast, and many have taken Ivorian citizenship. The Lebanese immigrated to Ivory Coast in the late 19th and early 20th centuries, fleeing economic hardship in Lebanon, which was then under the control of the Ottoman Empire. Some of the Lebanese boarded ships thinking that they were headed to the United States, only to be left on the coast of West Africa by unscrupulous ship captains. Today, they and their descendents are primarily merchants and traders in Abidjan and other cities. They have not always lived in peace: during periods of unrest and economic difficulty, the Lebanese frequently have been subject to attack because of their relative wealth compared to the rest of the population. About 20,000 French also live in Ivory Coast. Many work as consultants or advisors to Ivorian government agencies.

Virtually all residents of Ivory Coast speak French, which is also the language used in all schools. In addition, most Ivorians know one or more of the many languages and dialects spoken by the various groups that make up the country. Among the more common languages spoken are Baoulé, which is spoken by over two million people; Senoufo, spoken by over one million; Dan, spoken by around 800,000; and Dioula, spoken by around 500,000. Dioula is also widely used in markets and among traders. Some of Ivory Coast's other languages are spoken by only a few thousand people.

Ethnic Conflict

During periods in which Ivory Coast's economy was booming, hundreds of thousands of workers from neighboring countries crossed the border into Ivory Coast looking for jobs. They would often stay with Ivorian relatives who were members of the same ethnic group. The presence of these foreign migratory workers has been a source of tension at times. During hard economic times, some Ivorians have blamed these foreign workers for the shortage of jobs.

"The notion of 'ivoirité' or 'ivoirianness' started out as a political tactic of former President Konan Bédié to prohibit some politicians, including prominent northerner Alassane Ouattara, from running for President," noted the international human-rights organization Refugees International in 2003. "It has increased tensions among ethnic groups and created a division between the mainly Muslim north, which is where most of those considered 'foreigners' are living, and the mainly Christian south."

Hostility against immigrant workers has at times been expressed violently. For example, in November 1999 15,000 Burkinabés (residents of Burkina Faso) were chased from their homes in the southwestern town of Tabou. After civil war broke out in Ivory Coast in the fall of 2002, approximately 400,000 workers from Burkina Faso, Guinea, Liberia, and Mali fled the country to escape harassment and persecution.

Religious Diversity

About 40 percent of Ivorians are Muslims, and around 20 percent are Christian (either Roman Catholic or Protestant). The remainder of the population practices traditional African religions. These traditional religions, although they vary from one ethnic group to another, usually involve the worship of ancestors and the belief in natural spirits. Believers pray to their

(Top) Ivorians walk past a mosque in Abidjan. About 40 percent of the people in Ivory Coast follow Islam. (Left) Christians in Ivory Coast, who make up about 20 percent of the population, celebrate mass.

ancestors for guidance and protection, and practice various rituals to ward off evil. Some of these religious also incorporate elements from Christianity or Islam.

The Muslim population is centered in the northern part of Ivory Coast, the area where Muslim traders and missionaries from North Africa and the Middle East first made contact with Ivorians more than 700 years ago. Muslims also make up about one-third of the population of Abidjan.

Christianity first appeared in Ivory Coast in the 19th century with the arrival of the French. It appealed to educated Ivorians and to those who wished to adopt European culture.

Traditionally, Ivory Coast has been a very tolerant society, in which different religious communities have coexisted in peace. Ivorians generally have not adhered to the more extremist or fundamentalist forms of either Islam or Christianity. Unfortunately, the violence that broke out during the 2000 election has altered the tradition of religious tolerance. Many followers of Alassane Ouattara believed that he was prevented from running for president because he is a Muslim.

Education

The Ivorian educational system consists of six years of primary school, after which students receive a certificate indicating they have completed their primary studies. All Ivorian children are required to attend school through the primary years, although this law often is not enforced. This is followed by seven years of secondary school. The curriculum of both primary and secondary schools is based on French schools, and the language of instruction is French. Secondary school students also study English. Students who complete their studies receive a *baccalauréat*, which is the equivalent of a high-school diploma.

In addition to public schools, which are free through the secondary level, Ivory Coast has a number of private schools. Catholic schools are found mostly in the southern part of the country, where the Christian population is large, while in the north there are many Islamic schools that emphasize study of the *Qur'an*, Islam's holy scriptures.

The principal of a primary school in Bouake speaks to a first-grade class. All children in Ivory Coast must attend school through the primary grades—the equivalent of first through sixth grades in the United States.

Students who receive the *baccalauréat* are eligible to continue their education. The National University of Ivory Coast, which was established in 1958, was split into three separate universities in 1996. Two of them—the Université de Cocody and the Université d'Abobo-Adjamé—are located in Abidjan. The third, the Université de Bouaké, is in central Ivory Coast. In addition to the National University, there are several technical and teacher-training institutions that do not require a *baccalauréat* to enroll.

Some upper-class Ivorians have traditionally gone overseas to study, primarily to France, Germany, or the United States. Some have returned to Ivory Coast, but many others have sought employment opportunities in Europe or the United States. At the same time, many students from other African countries travel to Ivory Coast to study at the national university.

The government of Ivory Coast traditionally has devoted substantial funds to its educational system. At independence in 1960, only a small proportion of the Ivorian population was **literate**, but by 2003 more than 50 percent of the total population could read and write. However, Ivory Coast's literacy rate remains among the world's lowest, and further improvement will depend upon the availability of financial resources to pay for more schools and teachers.

The Arts and Music

Ivorians have produced some of the best examples of one of Africa's greatest art forms: the carved wooden mask. Each ethnic group has its own artistic style, but masks made by the Baoulé, Dan, and Senoufo people are regarded as the finest. Dancers or spiritual leaders wear the masks in a variety of religious ceremonies.

Some of the best examples of Ivorian carved masks are in museums throughout the world and bring high prices at international auctions. Such prominent western artists as Pablo Picasso, Henri Matisse, and Amedeo Modigliani were strongly influenced by the sometimes-abstract faces and figures on West African masks. When Picasso first encountered African masks

Carved Baoulé masks like this one fulfill the Baoulé ideal of beauty. The finest of these masks are prized as great art, and influenced such European artists as Pablo Picasso and Henri Matisse.

at a Paris gallery in 1907, he was amazed. "The masks weren't just like any other pieces of sculpture," he said. "They were magic things."

Music and dance are an important part of Ivorian culture. Most of Ivory Coast's ethnic groups have their own unique musical traditions and styles. Music, song, and dance are an integral part of religious celebrations, such as weddings and funerals. The Dan, who live in western Ivory Coast, are especially known for their musical tradition.

Abidjan today is regarded as the musical capital for all of West Africa, and musicians from throughout the region come to Abidjan to perform their own music as well as to hear the sounds of other cultures. The city teems with clubs and music halls. Abidjan's recording industry is one of the most sophisticated in Africa and attracts musicians from as far away as Congo. Ivorians are thus exposed to a great diversity of African musical styles, and it is not uncommon to hear music in many different languages on Ivorian radio stations.

The first Ivorian musician to gain widespread recognition was Ernesto Djedje. In the early 1960s, he began to combine various elements of traditional Ivorian ethnic music with the musical style of neighboring states. The result was a new—and purely Ivorian—style of music known as *ziglibithy*. Djedje was wildly popular until his death in 1983.

Ivory Coast's most famous musician, however, is Alpha Blondy, who has won worldwide recognition as Africa's greatest reggae musician. Although reggae is a musical form that developed in Jamaica, it gained popularity in Africa during the 1980s. Blondy grew up in an Ivorian village that was home to several different ethnic groups and to both Christians and Muslims. This multicultural environment made him open to people of all backgrounds. When as a teenager he first started exploring reggae music and Jamaican culture, his parents feared he was crazy, and actually sent him to a psychiatric hospital. He later attended Columbia University in New York to study English, but while there met a number of Jamaican reggae musicians. When he returned to Ivory Coast he started recording reggae music. Before long, he was asked to perform on Ivorian television, and soon was playing before packed audiences in Africa and Europe. Blondy's music has a unique sound and is clearly influenced by the African music that he heard as a child. His music also reflects his worldly views and his tolerance of all people. He has recorded songs in Dioula (his native language), English, French, Hebrew, and Arabic.

Alpha Blondy, Ivory Coast's most famous musician, performs at a concert.

Literature in Ivory Coast

Prior to the introduction of written European languages, most African societies preserved their cultural heritage through stories, legends, poems, and songs that were passed down orally from one generation to another. By the early 20th century, many of these stories were collected and translated into French by such writers as François Joseph Amon d'Aby and Marius Ano N'guessan.

An Ivorian writer named Benard Dadié also set out to translate these stories, and in the process he became Ivory Coast's most prominent author. Dadié was born in 1916 in a small coastal town in Ivory Coast. He was educated at Catholic schools, where he learned French. He studied and worked in Senegal for ten years before returning to Abidjan in 1947 to write for a newspaper. He also was active in the independence movement, and spent more than a year in prison because of his pro-independence activities. In 1953, he published *African Legends*, a French translation of some of his favorite African tales. His 1954 collection of African stories, *The Black Cloth*, was also translated into English. Many of the ancient tales and legends Dadié recorded are about Ananze the Spider, a traditional and humorous character in stories throughout West Africa. Dadié also wrote original poetry and an autobiography about his childhood in colonial Ivory Coast, as well as several plays and novels.

Dadié has been widely recognized for his accomplishments. When Ivory Coast became independent he served in the new government as minister of culture and information. In 2004, the Ivorian Publishers Association created the Bernard Dadié Prize for African Literature, to be awarded annually to an accomplished African author.

Other important writers from Ivory Coast include Ahmadou Kourouma, Jean-Marie Adiaffi, Isaïe Biton Koulibaly, Zegoua Gbessi Nokan, Tidiane Dem, Amadou Kone, Grobli Zirignon, Paul Yao Akoto, and Jérôme Carlos Maurice Bandaman. Women who have contributed greatly to the country's literary reputation include Simone Kaya, Fatou Bolli, Regina Yaou, Tanella Boni, Anne-Marie Adiaffi, Véronique Tadjo, Flore Hazoumé, Gina Dick, and Jeanne de Cavally.

(Opposite) The skyline of Abidjan, Ivory Coast's largest city. Abidjan is the center of the country's commerce. (Right) The enormous Basilica of Our Lady of Peace is modeled on St. Peter's Basilica in Rome. This church in Yamoussoukro is one of the largest Christian churches in the world, and can seat 7,000 worshippers.

6 The Communities of Ivory Coast

NEARLY 45 PERCENT of Ivory Coast's 16 million people live in cities, and the rate is increasing every year as people migrate from rural areas in search of jobs and opportunities. Among Ivory Coast's fascinating cities are modern and cosmopolitan Abidjan, the stunning capital city of Yamoussoukro, and the interior market town of Bouaké.

Abidjan

With a population of 3.5 millon, Abidjan is Ivory Coast's largest city and the country's business and commercial center. Many government agencies are also located in Abidjan, even though it has not been the country's capital since 1983.

Abidjan's natural setting is stunning. It is built around several lagoons and inlets on a series of islands and peninsulas, connected to one another by bridges. It boasts the largest port in all of West Africa, and its downtown area—known as "the plateau"—has some of Africa's tallest skyscrapers. The Hotel Ivoire, located on a lagoon facing downtown, is regarded as the grandest hotel in West Africa.

Abidjan is a young city. As recently as 1900, it was only a small and insignificant fishing village. In 1904, it became the *terminus* of a railroad line that the French built into the interior of the country, and in 1934 it was made the colonial capital. But its growth really took off in 1951 when the French constructed a canal to connect the city with the Atlantic Ocean, thus making Abidjan a port. Before long, it had become the commercial and shipping hub for much of West Africa, especially the *landlocked* countries such as Mali that had no outlets to the sea. When Ivory Coast became independent in 1960, it was the natural choice as capital.

Abidjan's population is diverse, and includes members of all of Ivory Coast's major ethnic groups, migrant workers from neighboring countries, and a large community of French and Lebanese. Restaurants serve everything from classic French and Italian cuisine, Lebanese dishes, and traditional African food. Because of its sophisticated and cosmopolitan atmosphere, Abidjan is sometimes referred to as the "Paris of Africa." Its nightlife and music clubs are famous, and its large student population gives the city a youthful energy to mix with the more serious government bureaucrats and bankers.

Some neighborhoods of Abidjan, such as Cocody, have beautiful homes, fancy restaurants, and exclusive shops. The Treichville neighborhood is home to a huge indoor market, where shoppers bargain with merchants for everything from exquisite African art and textiles to pots and pans.

Despite Abidjan's outward glamour, many of the city's residents live in squalid slums on the edges of the gleaming downtown, and crime has been a serious problem in recent years. Many of the city's wealthiest residents hire armed guards to protect their expensive homes and businesses.

Yamoussoukro

Before 1980, Yamoussoukro was a small town of only 25,000 people, the majority of whom were Baoulé. But it happened to be the hometown of Ivory Coast's first president, Félix Houphouet-Boigny, and he launched a massive and expensive program to turn the small town into the country's official capital in 1983. He not only built new a new presidential palace complex and offices for government agencies, but he also spent millions of dollars to construct hotels, an airport, apartment buildings for government employees, schools, and a modern freeway connecting Yamoussoukro to Abidjan, 125 miles (201 km) to the south.

But Houphouet-Boigny's grandest project in Yamoussoukro was the construction of the Basilica of Our Lady of Peace, the largest Christian church in the world. Built in just three years at a cost of $300 million, and soaring nearly 500 feet (150 m) at its highest, the basilica is larger than St. Peter's Basilica in Rome. Its pews can seat 7,000 people, and 300,000 people can pack into its courtyard. The basilica was dedicated by Pope John Paul II in a lavish ceremony in 1990 that attracted hundreds of dignitaries from around the world.

Today, Yamoussoukro is home to around 300,000 people, many of whom work for the government or for the tourist industry that caters to Christian religious pilgrims from throughout Africa who come to visit the cathedral.

Bouaké

Located in central Ivory Coast, Bouaké is a major market city for a region that produces coffee, cotton, palm oil, and other commodities. Its grand market is one of the best in West Africa, with merchants selling artwork, traditional African clothing, and an abundance of fruits and vegetables.

Bouaké has a population of around 550,000 and is Ivory Coast's second-largest city. It was first settled in the late 1890s as a French military outpost, and grew after the French built the railroad line to Mali. Its location on the railroad line about midway between Abidjan and Bamako, the capital of Mali, has made it a transportation and freight hub. Bouaké has several cotton mills, as well as important government-run technical schools in forestry and veterinary science. It also is the administrative capital of a large region of central Ivory Coast.

Grand Bassam

One of the most interesting towns in Ivory Coast is Grand Bassam (population 86,000), the first French colonial capital of Ivory Coast. Although Grand Bassam was the capital for only six years (from 1893 to 1899), during this period the French built a number of impressive buildings in the area of town now known as "Old Bassam," including a governor's house, courthouse, and post office. A severe outbreak of deadly yellow fever in 1899 forced the French to move the capital to the town of Bingerville, which is further inland.

Today, the seaside ruins of the French colonial buildings evoke another era. Many of the buildings are being renovated as tourist attractions. The beach at Grand Bassam is a favorite destination of residents of Abidjan, a mere 28 miles (45 kilometers) away. It is lined with small hotels and restaurants, and on weekends and holidays the highway between Abidjan and Grand Bassam is jammed with traffic.

Korhogo

With a population of around 165,000, Korhogo is one of the largest cities in the arid and hot northern part of Ivory Coast. Korhogo is an ancient town, settled in the 14th century by a chief of the Senoufo people. It remains

This building in Grand Bassam dates from the colonial period.

a center of Senoufo life and culture, and many of the surrounding villages specialize in traditional artwork and crafts of the Senoufo. The most famous product is korhogo cloth—woven and beautifully decorated cotton textiles that are used for everything from bedspreads to napkins. Korhogo is also a major trading center for local farmers, who come to town to sell their corn, millet, and yams in a market at the center of town.

A Calendar of Ivorian Festivals

Because of Ivory Coast's ethnic and religious diversity, nearly every week brings a celebration, festival, or religious holiday. Some festivals are celebrated only by certain ethnic or religious groups; others have been adopted by the entire nation. Many of the traditional festivals are a treat to the senses, featuring music, dancing, and colorful exotic costumes. The major holidays of Islam and Christianity, the two principal religions of Ivory Coast, are recognized as official holidays by the government.

The major Muslim holidays are based on a lunar calendar, which means that each year they are held 11 days earlier than the year before. Thus, any Muslim holiday could be celebrated during any month of the Western calendar. In the descriptions below, Muslim holidays are described during the month in which they occured in 2004.

January

New Year's Day is celebrated in most parts of Ivory Coast with revelry, much as it is in the rest of the world. Areas with a large Muslim population, however, are less like to celebrate New Year's in January, because the Muslim calendar has a separate New Year holiday that varies from year to year.

February

Fetes des Masques (Festival of Masks) is a holiday celebrated by members of the Dan ethnic group, centered in the western Ivorian city of Man and villages in the area. The Dan are widely known for their incredibly beautiful and elaborate carved wooden masks, and this annual festival brings together Dan mask-makers from throughout the region. The city of Man comes to life with masked dancers, musicians and other performances.

Eid al-Adha, or Feast of the Sacrifice, is held during the last month of the Islamic lunar calendar. This holiday celebrates Abraham's willingness to sacrifice his son for God, and many Muslims commemorate it by sacrificing a lamb, which they traditionally share with the poor. The Muslim New Year is celebrated on the first day of the following month, known as **Muharram**.

March

Le Carnaval de Bouaké (the Carnival of Bouaké), which began in 1964, has become one of Africa's largest festivities. It is an opportunity for the residents of Bouaké to show off their city and its culture. The carnival includes musical performances, culinary events, and an agricultural fair to showcase the region's rich and varied agricultural products. The carnival has become a national event, and government officials from Yamoussoukro and Abidjan usually attend some of the activities.

April

Easter is an important religious holiday for Ivory Coast's Christian community, and the churches and cathedrals are usually filled to capacity. Easter Monday is also a holiday.

A Calendar of Ivorian Festivals

Fete du Dipri is an annual event held in the village of Gomon, not far from Abidjan. Based on ancient traditions, the festival starts at midnight, when women and children walk through the village naked to ceremoniously rid it of evil spirits. At sunrise, the village chief appears, musicians perform, and for the rest of the day villagers celebrate with food and masked dancing.

May

Like much of the world, Ivoirians celebrate **Labor Day** as a public holiday on May 1. Offices and schools are closed.

Mawlid al-Nabiy, the commemoration of the birthday of the Prophet Mohammed, is celebrated by prayer and often a procession to the local mosque.

August

August 7 is Ivory Coast's **Independence Day**, celebrated with speeches and other patriotic activities.

August 15 is **Assumption Day**, a Christian holiday celebrating the Virgin Mary's ascent into heaven.

October

Ramadan is a month-long Muslim holiday during which devout Muslims fast and pray throughout the daylight hours. It is the holiest period in Islam. As soon as the sun goes down, families and friends gather in homes for a meal denoting the end of the fasting day. At the end of Ramadan, Muslims celebrate a major holiday called **Eid al-Fitr**—the Festival of the Breaking of the Fast. This is a joyous time characterized by feasts and family gatherings; children often receive gifts.

Fete de l'Abissa is a week-long carnival held in the former colonial capital and beach resort of Grand Bassam.

November

November 1 is **All Saints' Day**, a Christian holiday honoring all of the Church's saints, even those whose names will never be known. It is a day of prayer and church services.

December

December 7 is **Felix Houphouet-Boigny Remembrance Day**, a holiday devoted to celebrating the life and historical importance of Ivory Coast's first president (prior to Houphouet-Boigny's death in 1993, this date was celebrated as National Day).

Ivory Coast's Christians celebrate **Christmas Day** with church services and family gatherings. It also is a national holiday for all Ivorians.

Recipes

Kedjenou

1 whole chicken
1 eggplant, cut in pieces
2 large onions, minced
2 fresh hot peppers, seeded, and minced
4 tomatoes, peeled, seeded, and crushed
1 small piece ginger root, grated
1 sprig of thyme
1 bay leaf
salt to taste

Directions:
1. Clean the chicken and cut it in pieces.
2. Place the cut-up chicken and all the other ingredients in a large pot with a tight-fitting lid.
3. Cook over medium heat for about 45 minutes, stirring periodically to prevent sticking.

Ivorian Fish

2 cups yellow onion, chopped finely
1 teaspoon crushed red pepper
1 tablespoon salt
1 teaspoon pepper
4 oz. peanut or canola oil
2 lbs. pumpkin or yellow squash, cut into 1 inch slices
2-1/2 lbs. white ocean fish filet, such as halibut, cut into 1/2- to 3/4-inch slices
1 cup shredded coconut
2 cups white rice
1 6-oz. can tomato paste

Directions:
1. In a 6-quart Dutch oven or casserole baking dish, sauté in oil the onions with the crushed red pepper, salt, and black pepper until onions are soft but not brown.
2. Place pumpkin or squash pieces over the onions.
3. Place fish pieces over the pumpkin or squash.
4. Sprinkle coconut over fish.
5. Pour white rice, uncooked, over the coconut.
6. Carefully pour in 2 quarts of water and tomato paste.
7. Cover tightly and cook over medium heat for 30 minutes or until fish, rice and vegetables are tender. Serve from casserole dish.

Meat with Sauce Arachide

1/2 cup peanut butter
4 whole pimento peppers
18 cherry tomatoes, crushed
beef, chicken, or fish pieces (pre-cooked)
1 tablespoon of salt
1 tablespoon peanut or canola oil
1/2 small onion, mashed

Directions:
1. Place peanut butter in a small pot and slowly add about 1 cup of water. Mix well with hands until peanut butter and water are thoroughly combined.
2. Bring the peanut sauce to a boil and add 2 cups of water over a 30-minute period.
3. Add 4 whole pimento peppers.
4. Add 12 mashed cherry tomatoes and more water; continue to boil for 50 minutes.
5. Add 2-1/2 cups of water, and return to boil for 20 minutes.
6. Add pre-cooked meat of choice and 1 tablespoon of salt.
7. Boil for 35 minutes.
8. Add 6 more mashed cherry tomatoes, 1 tablespoon of oil, and mashed onion.
9. Let boil at least another 15 minutes, then serve.

Chilled Avocado Soup

2 very ripe avocados
4 cups cold chicken or vegetable stock
2 tablespoons lime juice
1 tablespoon plain yoghurt
2 dashes of Tabasco sauce
salt and black pepper to taste

Directions:
1. Peel avocados and remove pit. Place avocado flesh in a blender and puree.
2. Add chicken or vegetable stock and puree until smooth.
3. Blend in other ingredients.
4. Chill for one hour before serving.

Glossary

appeal—in law, to request that a higher court review a lower court's ruling.

authoritarian—a form of government in which power is concentrated in a leader or small group of leaders.

autonomous—having the right of self-government.

biodiversity—the number of different species of plants and animals.

cabinet—a group of government officials and advisors.

charismatic—having great personal attraction to other people.

delineate—to define or designate a boundary.

diversify—to increase variety.

equator—on maps, the invisible line around the middle of the earth that is equally distant from the north and south poles.

ethnic group—people of the same racial background who share a common culture or tradition.

faction—a political party or group, usually in opposition to other groups.

gross domestic product (GDP)—the total value of goods and services produced by a country in a single year.

hydroelectric—a method of generating electricity by using water power from dammed rivers.

indigenous—originating in or native to a particular area.

infrastructure—the basic framework of public works, such as water and sewer systems, roads, and telephone lines, within a country.

lagoon—a shallow body of water connected to a nearby larger body of water.

Glossary

landlocked—having no access to the sea.

linguistic—pertaining to languages.

literate—able to read and write.

migrate—to move from one country or region to another.

mission—a center run by a religious or charitable organization offering food, shelter, aid, and spiritual comfort to needy people.

plantation—a large independent farm employing many workers.

plateau—an extensive area of land with a flat surface that is somewhat higher than surrounding land areas.

prefect—an appointed government official in charge of an area or region.

Qur'an—the holy book of the Islamic religion.

referendum—a system of political decision-making in which the population votes on whether or not to adopt a proposed new policy.

savanna—a tropical grassland containing few trees.

socialist—a person who advocates socialism, which is a form of government in which the state controls resources of production, such as factories.

subsistence—a form of agriculture in which families grow just enough food to provide for their own needs.

terminus—the end of a route or transportation line.

unicameral—having a single legislative chamber.

Project and Report Ideas

Crafts

Research the various types of masks made by the different ethnic groups of Ivory Coast, and then make your own African mask using construction paper and other materials.

French Empire in Africa

France once controlled much of West Africa, including Ivory Coast. Draw a map of Africa, indicating which modern countries were once part of the French Empire. Investigate the ways in which France influenced the African societies it ruled over (for example, by imparting the French language).

Research project

Choose one of Ivory Coast's major ethnic groups, and prepare a report or poster on its traditions, history, and culture. Show on a map the areas of Africa in which the group lives.

Travel Guide

Prepare a brief travel guide to Ivory Coast highlighting the many sites that tourist should visit. Surf the Internet to find hotels and airlines that serve Ivory Coast. How easy is it to travel to Ivory Coast? What is the best way to travel inside the country?

Project and Report Ideas

Environmental challenges

Ivory Coast has lost most of its rainforest. Research rainforests and their importance to the ecosystem. Explain why the rainforests are threatened, and what countries can do to protect the remaining rainforests.

Commodities

Many countries in the developing world, such as Ivory Coast, are economically dependent upon the sale of commodities. Choose a commodity—such as coffee, sugar or cocoa—and find out 1) what its current price is on the international market, 2) how its price has fluctuated over the past several years, and 3) the five top producers of that commodity.

Chronology

11th century	Muslim traders make initial contacts with people living in what will become northern Ivory Coast.
ca. 1450	Portuguese explorers land in Ivory Coast, but do not establish permanent settlements.
ca. 1600	Various ethnic groups from neighboring areas begin migration into Ivory Coast.
ca. 1840	French begin building forts and settlements along the coast of Ivory Coast.
1885	European powers decide how to carve up Africa; France is granted control over Ivory Coast.
1893	Ivory Coast officially becomes a French colony.
1898	France defeats Malinke forces under Samory Touré in western Ivory Coast to secure its hold over the country.
1944	Félix Houphouet-Boigny forms a union of Ivorian farmers to protest against French policies.
1945	Houphouet-Boigny is elected to the French parliament, where he speaks out against colonialism.
1958	Ivory Coast becomes an autonomous republic within the French Community.
1960	Ivory Coast declares its full independence, and Houphouet-Boigny becomes the country's first president.
1979	Ivory Coast becomes the world's leading producer of cocoa.
1983	The capital is moved to Yamoussoukro.
1990	Ivory Coast holds its first multi-party elections; Houphouet-Boigny is reelected with 85 percent of the vote.

Chronology

1993   President Houphouet-Boigny dies; Henri Konan Bédié becomes president.

1999   Military coup led by General Robert Gueï ousts Bédié as president.

2000   Laurent Gbagbo elected president in controversial election.

2002   Civil strife breaks out, leading to widespread violence among various ethinc and religious groups.

2003   Government and rebel leaders agree to a truce in January, but in September the rebels pull out of the agreement.

2004   The United Nations sends a peacekeeping force to Ivory Coast to help maintain the truce and restore calm to the country.

Further Reading/Internet Resources

Arkhurst, Joy Cooper. *The Adventures of Spider: West African Folk Tales*. Boston: Little, Brown and Company, 1992.

Brownlie, Alison. *West Africa*. Austin, Texas: Raintree/Steck Vaughn, 1999.

Dedie, Bernard. *The Black Cloth: A Collection of African Folk Tales*. Amherst: University of Massachusetts Press, 1987.

Hamilton, Janice. *Ivory Coast in Pictures*. Minneapolis: Lerner Publications, 2004.

Merrill, Yvonne and Mary Simpson. *Hands-On Africa: Art Activities for All Ages Featuring Sub-Saharan Africa.* Salt Lake City: Kits Publishing, 2000.

History and Geography

http://www.sas.upenn.edu/African_Studies/Country_Specific/Cote.html
http://www.state.gov/r/pa/ei/bgn/2846.htm

Economic and Political Information

http://www.sas.upenn.edu/African_Studies/Country_Specific/Cote.html
http://www.presidence.gov.ci/
http://www.alertnet.org/thefacts/countryprofiles/216639.htm
http://www.mbendi.co.za/land/af/ci/p0005.htm

Culture and Festivals

http://www.friendsofcotedivoire.org/
http://www.sas.upenn.edu/African_Studies/NEH/u-ethn.html

Travel Information

http://www.abidjan.com
http://www.africaguide.com/

United States Embassy in Ivory Coast
Rue Jesse Owens
01 B.P. 1712
Abidjan, Ivory Coast
(225) 20-21-09-79
http://usembassy.state.gov/abidjan/

Embassy of the Republic of Ivory Coast
2424 Massachusetts Avenue, NW
Washington, DC 20008
(202) 797-0300

Index

Numbers in **bold italics** refer to captions.

Index

Contributors/Picture Credits

Professor Robert I. Rotberg is Director of the Program on Intrastate Conflict and Conflict Resolution at the Kennedy School, Harvard University, and President of the World Peace Foundation. He is the author of a number of books and articles on Africa, including *A Political History of Tropical Africa* and *Ending Autocracy, Enabling Democracy: The Tribulations of Southern Africa*.

William Mark Habeeb is a professor and international affairs consultant in Washington, D.C. He has written widely on such topics as international negotiation, the politics and culture of North African states, and the Arab-Israeli conflict. He received his Ph.D. in international relations from the Johns Hopkins University School of Advanced International Studies.